Fanning the Flame:

Notes from Pastors to Pastors

Edited by Michael L. Ehret

MMA®

Stewardship Solutions

Goshen, Indiana

Fanning the Flame

Book design by Alicia Beam

MMA®

Stewardship Solutions

1110 North Main Street
Post Office Box 483
Goshen, IN 46527

Toll-free: (800) 348-7468
Telephone: (574) 533-9511
www.mma-online.org

Contents

Striking the match:
Nurturing yourself

Ministry begins with prayer

By Truman Brunk

My prayer life was founded on experiences of answered childhood prayer. My mother was a praying woman. I remember one evening after a very busy day on the farm, my father came to the house lamenting that he had lost his billfold. As a child only eight years old, I went to my bed, knelt down, and prayed, "Lord, please show me where Dad's billfold is." I felt like I received an answer, so I went to my father and said, "Dad, let's go out to the field."

We began walking over those 38 acres of newly plowed ground. I kicked against a clod, and uncovered the wallet! It was a miracle, and I began to believe in a great God.

God listens to children. And to a childlike prayer. His walls are thin. He lets the door open. He wants to pour out his answers if we would only ask.

Later in life, when in crisis or in a painful situation, I learned to practice "centering prayer." I find a Scripture that speaks into the circumstance, then repeat it over and over until God responds. For example, Psalm 51:1, "Have mercy upon me, O God," is a prayer I repeat over and over and over – and surprises follow!

On one occasion, I was stricken with a severe case of Bells Palsy in my face, so severe I could hardly speak. The neurologist told me, "You will battle that for years." I cried out, "Have mercy upon me, O God!" I repeated it over and over – 50, 500, 5,000 times. God healed me in 10 days! It was as powerful a healing as the Apostle Paul on the Damascus Road. I felt hit over the head by the grace of God. "My grace is sufficient for you for my power is made perfect in weakness." (2 Corinthians 12:9)

There are so many demands on you as a pastor. So many demands for your time that there is often little time left for prayer. However, ministry begins with prayer. A pastor who prays is, in effect, saying, "less of myself and more of God." It isn't great faith that answers prayer – but a great God. Even a tiny little faith in a great God! "Ask and it shall be given ..." (Luke 11:9)

Blessings,

Truman

Scriptures: Luke 11:9; 2 Corinthians 12:9.

Truman Brunk is an overseer in the Virginia Conference of Mennonite Church USA. He has served as a pastor for more than 30 years in Virginia and Pennsylvania.

True friendship

By Gregory D. Getz

I came to a new town and a new church as a staff person assigned to start a new church plant. Fortunately, I had one friend already on location who became part of our planting core group. Obviously, everyone else was a stranger unless I decided to make him or her a friend. My wife and I opened our home frequently, inviting people over for the express purpose of getting to know them. More and more people chose to join the core group for the new church, and we bonded quickly around a common vision and task. In many ways, it was a very mission-oriented small group, and we had a lot of fun.

That experience is different from the typical pastor who comes to a new church, but finds he and his family are on the outside looking in at a congregation with well-established friendships and cliques. Friends among the congregation are often either unconnected parishioners or people who dutifully expand their relational base along the context of church business. Making friends in such situations can be so tough you may be inclined to withdraw to the small but friendly confines of the immediate family. But remember why you are there — to serve and to lead that congregation. You can do both better from a platform of true friendship.

What is true friendship? I have learned to distinguish between colleagues, coworkers, acquaintances, and (true) friends. Only true friends can be trusted, and they are as rare and beautiful as the blue diamond or the double rainbow. Only the true friend will appreciate your tears, tell you your bad joke is not funny, and be safe enough to share your intimate struggles of marriage, temptation, or self-esteem with. Anything less may be nice, but it's not a friend.

Due to the exquisiteness of true friendship, it does require a certain amount of nurturing. Now, I'm not talking about the high maintenance of a pseudo-friendship, but rather shared experiences that have nostalgic qualities. Ministry times, vacations, work, extended shared family, overnight conferences, personal tragedy, and education challenges are all experiences I've shared with true friends – and we still laugh and cry about them. But more importantly they are like bookmarks in a biography – a place where we pick up together and proceed with the story. Learn to understand the importance of these shared experiences, and become alert to future experience opportunities that will strengthen the bonds with your true friends.

Whether your true friendships are nourished through phone calls, personal visits, e-mails, or other means is not as important as the message. The primary message in a true friendship is, "I care more about what's happening in your life than I care about mine." That's not to say you don't get to share your life, because a true friend has the same philosophy and will eagerly inquire about what is special to you. The net result is the unselfish sharing of life – no one keeping score – with no strings attached (manipulation) and no needs demanded to be met (selfishness).

Consider taking a risk and breaking out of your routine circles of people and activities! Join a health club, buy a motorcycle, stop and stay for coffee at the same place every Saturday morning, volunteer for your subdivision board – or any other activity that puts you in close proximity to people who share your (new!) activity. Most of all, make the greatest effort to circulate with unchurched people. If you cannot develop friendships with them, you cannot preach with relevance to them.

Speaking of preaching, when you do, share your life. You will be amazed at how people will open their hearts, homes, and schedules to include you. As you begin a journey of friendship, make it true friendship – first by being a student of their life and then, when they eagerly and genuinely ask, being open with your own life joys, fears, and tears. Don't be a (professional!) pastor to them; instead share your life with them. That's risky – but it's a risk worth taking!

Blessings,

Greg

Scriptures: Proverbs 17:17, 18:24, 27:17; Ecclesiastes 4:9-10; John 15:13.

Rev. Gregory D. Getz is the coordinator of the Missionary Church's Pastoral Leadership Institute, which trains second-career pastors for ministry.

Enlarge your world

By Dr. David L. Hall

The thrill of discovering new insights spurred me to continue my formal education. While serving as a teacher/administrator, I enrolled in a master's program with the idea of pursuing a Ph.D. Later, I accepted a call to full-time pastoral ministry with the condition I be allowed time for formal study.

Studying at a Catholic university with an interdenominational group of graduate students allowed me to have a rich mixture of ideas, traditions, and experiences to bring to my pastoral work. The pastorate informed my study and served to stimulate other students and professors. Pastoral work forced me to continually assess the value and applicability of academic theory, while the pastorate kept my feet firmly planted in the pains and joys of life beyond academia.

The continual struggle to prioritize commitments of home, church, and school weighed heavily. The support of my family and church family, although many did not understand my needs and goals, were crucial to my continuing during times of discouragement and overcommitment. I became aware that no one continues his/her education without someone else making a sacrifice, even if it is only a short seminar.

From my Catholic and Lutheran friends, I learned something about the value of liturgy in worship. They, and many others, have enabled me to experience God's grace and love. I have learned I am human and that it is okay to be human. God expects no more or less.

I have learned I need input into my life beyond my world of pastoring. A pastor's world can become very small. I need input from a variety of sources – secular and spiritual. I need to continue to be a lifelong learner in mundane things such as golf, because it may teach me eternal values – like humility. I have learned that no answers are final – they simply lead to more and better questions. The need to continue my education goes on.

During this period of my life I lived in the Psalms. They reflect all the emotions of my journey. They invite me to praise and worship in the difficult times and times of celebration.

I don't know exactly when Psalm 116 became my favorite. The first two verses, which reflect God's love and care for me, struck me one day as I was reading: "I am filled with love when Yahweh listens to the sound of my prayers. When he bends down to hear me as I call." (Psalm 116:1-2, New Jerusalem Bible). The image of God, my creator, bending down to listen to my prayers is incredible to me. All the concerns of life and pastoring seem to me to be addressed in this Psalm.

I held back tears as I stood near the checkout desk of the university library for the last time. I thought about all the books I hadn't read and how ignorant I really was. There was so much more to learn. My advice to you, pastor:

- Be a pastor who is a growing, learning being.
- Be teachable. Be willing to learn from anyone. God may show up in the words of a four-year-old as easily as in the words of Scripture.
- Try not to limit God.
- Be aware you are both learner and teacher. Knowing a lot doesn't make you a good pastor. Loving a lot does.
- Don't try to be something more than you are. Don't live out of others' expectations.
- Learn to be you. The you that God has made and called you to be and become.
- Hold on to your dreams.
- Above all, be honest with yourself.

The pastors I admire the most have been willing to be vulnerable, not perfect. I learned more about being a pastor from one nameless pastor's silence in a small group than from any words he could have spoken. I learned more about being a pastor from one pastor's tears than from four years of his preaching.

Learn to be. Doing is important, but it is not ultimate. What you are is more important than what you do.

Blessings,

David

Scripture: Psalm 116.

Dr. David L. Hall is senior pastor of Hartville (Ohio) Mennonite Church.

Surprised by God's word

By Keith Harder

The Scriptures have always been a powerful influence in my life, especially the Gospel accounts and the stories involving the early church. They continue to provide a fundamental point of orientation and an ongoing source of inspiration. At crucial moments in my life, they provided the impetus for changes in thinking and direction and provided a source of encouragement in times of deep distress.

Earlier in my life, when I thought I had pretty much figured out the biblical story, I tended to use the Bible more to support my views and to challenge others rather than letting it continue to challenge and change me. I have since come to a deeper appreciation of the whole Bible, especially those parts that at first glance seem alien and irrelevant to my life. I continue to learn how to listen to the text in its strangeness as well as how to invite it to confront my assumptions and ideas.

I will always read and interpret Scripture from my own particular point of view, which has been formed by a myriad of experiences and influences. You will do the same. This awareness compels me to recognize that I need to read and study Scripture with others, to hear and consider other perspectives and cultures, and to hear what others hear in the text. This is a benefit not easily dismissed. May I encourage you to do the same?

I have favorite Scriptures I return to again and again, but it is also important for me to expect God to speak to me from unexpected places in the Bible.

One final encouragement: Be alert to what you are bringing to the text. Open yourself to alternate understandings, and expect to be surprised by God's word.

Blessings,

Keith

Scripture: Matthew 14:52.

Keith Harder is director of the congregational and ministerial leadership team of Mennonite Church USA and has served as pastor of First Mennonite Church, Hillsboro, Kan.

Abounding in grace

By Wallace Jantz

My stress level was very high the first several years of my ministry because I had not done enough "inner work." Anxiety rooted in my early years was not resolved adequately, and some of the stress was due to a fear of conflict and financial anxiety.

Some of my motivation for ministry, unconscious at the time, was unearthed via counseling and I learned that we minister out of who we are. We can project more darkness than light when we have not processed our personal issues. But grace abounds when we are vulnerable; when we offer who we are to God and to those to whom we minister. I have also become more aware that God changes people – change is not a human endeavor!

If you are experiencing a lot of stress, you may want to consider finding a spiritual mentor/director. Pastors are only effective in ministering to others to the extent they are themselves ministered to. Other ways to reduce stress:

- Keep your priorities on track: 1. God/Jesus. 2. Spouse and family. 3. Ministry in the church.

- Consistent meditation, prayer, reading the Bible for personal enrichment – read widely.

- Specialize in self-care. Exercise, eat properly, enjoy music and the arts. Don't take yourself too seriously. Some humor is a must. Laugh at yourself; laugh with others.

- Develop a schedule your congregation can access.

- Develop a support group composed of people who are not in official roles in the church, a setting where you can be fully human.

Blessings,
Wallace

Scripture: Psalm 121; Psalm 90:1,2; John 14:27; Romans 8:31-38; Ephesians 1:8-10; Philippians 1:1-6; Philippians 4:4-7; 1 John 1:5-10; 1 Peter 5:7; and 2 Peter 5:7.

Wallace Jantz is a retired pastor and conference minister with Mennonite Church USA.

Drinking from the deeper well

By Elaine Maust

I step silently from one patch of moss to the next, as I follow the living stepping stones into the woods. The moist Mississippi air smells of comfort – like opening the door to my grandmother's kitchen. Alone! Relief washes over me. When did I learn to so love the quiet?

How did I go from the extroverted little girl who would not shut up, to this woman who craves solitude? Whether it's a moment alone in the car, a silent retreat beside the lake, or an instant in a crowd when I slip into my quiet heart, I have learned to love silence.

Solitude is the deep well, from which I draw focus and calm in the presence of disaster, grief, and pain. Without solitude I would only be another noisy person. Solitude pulses through me as I sit with a woman whose husband lies dead on the bed beside us. It takes command as I stand beside a hospital bed and take in my hands the face of someone overcome by pain. It is the voice that does not speak when there is nothing to say. In one of those amazing complexities of God, it is solitude that makes me fit to be around people.

Jeff Landis, our youth pastor at Jubilee, said that like Moses, the faces of preachers should glow in proportion to the time they spent alone with God the week before. I said, "Thank God that doesn't happen!" But the truth is, it does. The Israelites knew Moses had been with God because of the light on his face (Exodus 34:29-35). Our congregations know whether or not we have been with God. I do not go into solitude hoping for an epiphany that will make the congregation pick up their heads on Sunday morning. But in silence, the presence [of God?] soaks into my life.

My times alone with God have been dramatic, but not often so. Many are routine and unimpressive, yet together they compose the pattern of our relationship. I do not demand God speak to me. Craddock says, "God does not talk all the time." I have learned to like that about God. No chattering. Sometimes God speaks to me. Sometimes we are quiet together.

In an attempt to live like Jesus, I not only preach and heal, but sometimes I slip away, to pray and listen (Luke 5:15-16). Solitude has taught me to recognize The Voice. Now, even in a crowd, I sometimes feel the hand of the Holy Spirit on my arm, and The Voice, like a great aunt warning, "Be careful!"

In this life, I do business in the currency of sound and companionship. I have accepted that I cannot flee them any more than I can escape the excesses I am tempted to regarding money or food. But I will discipline the noise, the hurry, the worry, the planning, and the pushing — with regular times alone with God.

I look forward to going to heaven. I would like to bake rolls for the marriage supper of the lamb and play the tambourine as all the tribes praise God. But sometimes I wonder if it won't be, on the whole, too many people for me. For the most part, you will probably find me wandering down by the river, watching the fruit ripen on the tree of life, relieved and grateful to be — at last — completely alone with God.

Blessings,
Elaine

Scripture: Exodus 34:29-35; Luke 5:15-16.

Elaine Maust is co-pastor of Jubilee Mennonite Church, Meridian, Miss.

Sailing away from burnout

By Lynn A. Miller

Having read Jay Sanford's little book on avoiding "ministerial burnout," I put aside the idea that having a hobby was an escape route from overwork and plunged headlong into the stream of first-year ministry demands. My "off-time" that first year was spent in "catching up," trying to stay one step ahead of my congregation's demands of its new pastor. During the second and third year, all of my *non*-ministry time was spent finishing the house that the congregation had helped me start in a one-day building blitz.

It wasn't until the third year, when my house was built and my sense of being a pastor was fully developed, that I began thinking of anything that approached a "hobby." At that point I began building a wooden skiff in the workshop I had built in the house. When the skiff was finished, I began looking for a more ambitious project, and began the construction of a gaff-rigged sailboat that would be suitable for Great Lakes sailing. After two years of melting lead, steam-bending oak frames, gluing and nailing planks, and finishing the curved surfaces, I launched the RE-TREAT — an apropos name since it was a treat to build, it is a treat to sail, and if someone calls the office on my day off, the secretary can honestly say that the Pastor is "on retreat."

The only criticism I received while building my boat was from a vocal "well-intentioned dragon" in the congregation who said I should be resting on my day off instead of boat building, so that I would be "more able to better minister to the congregation the rest of the week." I responded by telling that person that what I did on my day off was my business, which was, perhaps, not the most diplomatic answer but certainly one that satisfied me.

My perspective now, as it was then, is that a hobby should be simply the development of another area of interest in a person's life, not an escape from professional stress. Hobbies will not prevent burnout. Rather, if they are *too* enjoyable, they might instead *increase* the dissatisfaction one has with one's job. Hobbies also can help you prevent your perspective on life from becoming increasingly narrow.

Being a person gifted by God with a mind filled with curiosity, I have never needed a "proof text" to justify doing anything. Therefore I did not look to the Scriptures for any encouragement or direction in the area of developing a hobby. But, looking back on it from the perspective of time, I suppose that Matthew 5:48, "Be ye perfect (whole, complete) as your Father in Heaven is perfect" will do. A pastor, whose whole life is ministry to others, seems to be fairly one-sided, not whole or complete at all.

It is not recorded that Jesus had a hobby, but it is recorded that the apostle Paul had a trade of tent making that he engaged in with Aquila and Priscilla in Corinth. And while he stayed with them, he not only was "reasoning in the synagogue every Sabbath," he was working with them in their common trade as well (Acts 18:2-4). Likewise, although Simon and Andrew left their nets to become "fishers of men," they continued to fish when the opportunity presented itself, including soon after the resurrection of their Lord (John 21:1-11).

A hobby started as an antidote to the troubles of your job or to prevent burnout will not do the trick. Burnout happens not because you don't have a hobby, but because you are in ministry for the wrong reason(s). A hobby entered into for these reasons will simply be a distraction for a while, not a cure. But a hobby engaged in because it is something that satisfies an area of interest in your life not covered in your job description will be an addition to your ability to minister, not a detriment. Do not, however, expect everyone you minister to, to understand that distinction. Maybe they need a hobby – other than watching you.

Blessings,

Lynn

Scripture: Matthew 5:48; Acts 18:2-4; John 21:1-11.

Lynn A. Miller is MMA's stewardship theologian and has served as a pastor in the Mennonite Church USA.

Unearthing hidden treasures

By Dr. Janet M. Peifer

In my early years of ministry, it seemed to me the only thing that was adding up was my years. Little else was happening. Others misunderstood my call to ministry and I had no role models as a woman. As a result, I experienced a significant amount of depression and grief *until* I began my formal studies in ministry at age 39. That was when my response to the call of God on my life placed me in the midst of people I call "God's oldest friends," and I found my welcoming place of ministry.

I now see older adults as a hidden treasure to be unearthed in the church and in the community. When we are following God's plan, no life experiences are wasted. It is important to know and understand this. My initial disappointment in waiting so long to begin my studies helped me understand others and gave me the ability to offer the ministry of presence, of "being there," when there are no rational answers to life's perplexities.

If you are struggling in this area as a pastor, perhaps you will find your answers in the Psalms, the Prophets, and the Gospels – as I did. Texts that are rich in encouragement and ripe with the treasures of the wisdom of the aged. In addition, remember that:

- You can wait on the Lord. God will give you the desires of your heart.
- You may have to be your own best friend, if needed, as you prepare for days when other friends are leaving this world through death or cognitive loss.

- Learning and serving need not end until the day of one's departure from this earth.

- You must mourn before you can be comforted.

Blessings,
Janet

Scriptures: Selected passages in Psalms, the Prophets, and the Gospels.

Dr. Janet M. Peifer, East Berlin, Pa., is a Brethren in Christ pastor serving as director of pastoral care at Messiah Village, Mechanicsburg, Pa. She is also assistant convener of the Wesleyan Holiness Women Clergy, International. Janet shares on aging and grief from her many years of experience with "God's oldest friends."

Combat stress with good health

By Mary Grace Shenk

Daily routines with my family gave me plenty of physical activity early on. It took a period of high stress related to church and ministry to challenge me to make some lifestyle changes that encompassed my physical, emotional, and spiritual well-being.

Over the years, I have learned that the work of pastor tends toward high stress. Because of varied congregational demands and expectations, I have found that I must take care of myself to be effective in working with and relating to others in my ministry. For years now, my routine has included a 25- to 30-minute walk and time for spiritual disciplines (scripture reading/reflection/prayer).

In addition, I have made dietary changes to include less meat, fewer sweets, and more fruits and vegetables. Then, to address my mental health, I try as often as possible to spend time with people who help me laugh and not take myself too seriously.

God and Jesus, of course, set the standard. After six days of creating the world, God rested on the seventh (Genesis 2:2). Jesus, too, modeled getting away from the crowd (and the stresses and demands they represent) with this invitation to his disciples in Mark 6:31 — "Come with me by yourselves to a quiet place and get some rest."

Also, throughout Scripture we are reminded to care for our bodies, which are intricately knitted together, fearfully and wonderfully made (Psalm 139:13-14) in God's image (Genesis 1:27), and a temple of the Holy Spirit (1 Corinthians 6:19). In fact, wellness and wholeness permeate Scripture.

So, how do you do this? How do you incorporate taking care of yourself? The same way you incorporate anything else you consider important – you schedule it. Schedule time for daily spiritual disciplines, physical exercise, rest, and reflection – this will pay off in more energy and focus for your ministry activities. Schedule time with people who are encouragers and who nurture your sense of humor and your lighter side. Build into your sabbatical time for recreation, hobbies, and simply "being."

Blessings,

Mary Grace

Scripture: Genesis 1:27, 2:2; Mark 6:31; Psalm 139:13-14; 1 Corinthians 6:19.

Mary Grace Shenk has been a pastor more than 17 years and is currently co-pastoring with her husband at Hebron Mennonite Church in Hagerstown, Md. She has three children and five grandchildren.

A hope rooted in God

By Duncan Smith

As is true for anyone entering the ministry, my early years were a time of learning. On the one hand, serving as a pastor was a wonderful and challenging call of God. On the other hand, there were those persistent doubts and fears. Doubts in my own skills and abilities – and fear that I would fail or not be up to this new role.

Looking back, I remember a lot of ups and downs – like being on a roller coaster. There were always new challenges and new experiences, but the learning curve was steep. I was learning new skills, gaining new relationships with people, and seeking to discern what it meant to be a person who provided a listening pastoral ear as well as leadership and guidance for a congregation. In the midst of it, I realized I was also learning a deeper trust in the God who had called me.

Even today, I still have times of doubt and fear, but I find my ministry is on a much more even keel. Part of this is experience and learning. I am more confident in my abilities and have a better sense of what might be coming at me. I am a better leader with a fuller understanding of congregational dynamics. However, over the years, I have learned more about my own strengths and limitations. This helps me relax, knowing that I do not have to, nor can I, do it all myself. There is a reason Scripture talks about the body of Christ and the use of different gifts – the faith community needs the use of all of them to be whole.

Most of the time, I now approach my doubts and fears with hope – a hope rooted in God. A hope that allows me to see beyond the immediate to something new or even a hope beyond what I cannot see. ("For in hope we were saved" – Romans 8:24-30). Where before I may have been limited by my fears or doubts, I am now able to see opportunity for my own growth and for the working of God's Spirit through me and the ministry I am involved in.

I will share three meaningful scriptures that encourage and guide me to this day:

- **Matthew 6: 25-34** speaks of God's provision for this world and me and reminds me to focus on the things of God. *"But strive first for the kingdom of God and his righteousness, and all these things will be given to you as well."*

- **Ephesians 4:12** reminds me I must live a life worthy of my calling. It also reminds me that my calling is to be a servant, *"…to equip the saints for ministry, for building up the body of Christ."*

- **Philippians 2:1-11** is a wonderful hymn that reminds me of who Christ is and to worship (in verses 6-11). While verses 1-5 are a practical guide for me in my relationships with others. When I wonder why I serve, I go to this passage and remember how Christ lived and died: *"Do nothing from selfish ambition or conceit…"*

If you are struggling with doubt and fear, there are many steps you can take. The first two suggestions I have mean you will need to take steps that require discipline and action:

1. **Meet with a mentor on a regular basis.** In my early years of ministry, it was important to spend time sharing and praying about my ministry with another more experienced person. Not only did I gain valuable perspective, but helpful guidance.

2. **Prayer and reading Scriptures.** Spiritual practices also help keep things in perspective. Allow room for God to work in your life.

3. **Find a way for self-reflection.** This will happen by doing numbers one and two, but there might be other ways as well, such as journaling or meeting with friends. Self-reflection will save you many ill-conceived ideas or missteps.

The next three have a little more to do with your attitude or inner life, but also relate to the first three.

1. **Don't take things personally.** It is not usually about you. Easier said than done, right? While I still do take things personally at times, I remind myself not to with the following saying: "I don't take things personally – even if they are meant that way."

2. **Your point of fear or doubt is really your point of growth.** These points are opportunities. Meet them with hope and courage. Finally, and most important, No. 3.

3. **Trust in God.** God has called you and will be with you. It might feel at times like you are leaning off a cliff and about to fall. Imagine God holding you and you will not fall. Hope is leaning into this kind of trust in God.

Blessings,
Duncan

Scripture: Romans 8:24-30; Matthew 6:25-34; Ephesians 4:12; Philippians 2:1-11.

Duncan Smith is a conference minister for the Pacific Northwest Mennonite Conference of Mennonite Church USA. His pastoral experience stretches from the wheatfields of eastern Washington to the streets of the Bronx, New York City.

Companions in the ministry

By Ervin R. Stutzman

"Get Mark and bring him with you, because he is helpful to me in my ministry. I sent Tychicus to Ephesus. When you come, bring the cloak that I left with Carpus at Troas, and my scrolls, especially the parchments." (2 Timothy 4:11-13)

As I read this Scripture from 2 Timothy, I visualize the Apostle Paul languishing in prison awaiting a likely death sentence from Caesar. His co-workers have abandoned him or have been sent to other locations. He feels very much alone and urges Timothy to come for a visit. He gives instructions regarding the things he longs for in prison – including his scrolls and parchments. To Paul, these writings are like companions in ministry and they bring him deep comfort. He feels lonely without them.

I understand Paul's desire for his books. Ever since I was a child, I have enjoyed the opportunity to read. As I explored God's call to ministry, I began collecting books for my library. One of my favorite activities is browsing at the local book fair, hunting for bargains and exploring new worlds. But it's not just books that I devour. My world of ministry expanded when I subscribed to denominational magazines. Now I receive many magazines at my home, including news periodicals. Sometimes I have struggled to read them all.

In school, whenever I was given a reading assignment, I thought I needed to read every word in a book in order to glean what I needed. But I have since learned discernment. I read more selectively now, skipping or skimming over some areas and scrutinizing others with great care. Sometimes when I read, I place a sticky note on the edge of the page beside a paragraph that catches my attention. When I'm finished reading the book, I often rely on these notes for sermon preparation.

It's not been easy for me to find all the time I'd like to read – especially commentaries or other study materials. But I found that reading is one of the best ways for me to replenish my stock of supplies for pastoral ministry. I discovered I could cover a lot more material when I set aside a certain time for reading each day, even if only 30 minutes. This practice enables me to move from "studying on the edge of desperation" to "preaching from the overflow."

Early in my pastoral ministry, I learned the importance of writing as a complement to reading. Like many of my peers in high school, I didn't really enjoy writing. But one day in college, a professor quoted the famous line declaring "the pen is mightier than the sword." The phrase stuck with me. I have come to believe it — and apply it — in my own ministry.

Perhaps the most important person to write for is you — in the form of a journal. I've kept a journal for many years with different sections that relate to different areas of my life — family, pastoral ministry, spiritual insights, new ideas, etc. Once a month, on a prayer and planning day, I read the things I've written from the past month. These entries serve as reminders of the way God has enabled me through various struggles. They also reveal patterns of life I might otherwise fail to notice. Without reminders like these, I too readily forget important lessons God has taught me.

After I learned the importance of writing for myself, I expanded my audience to include others. Each year I write articles for a devotional magazine and have also written several books. As a pastor, you may have the opportunity to preach regularly. But you can add another dimension to your ministry if you do some writing — and you don't have to be a Max Lucado to have an impact. The simplest way to begin is to write letters or notes of affirmation and encouragement to members of your church. This is the kind of material people may pass on to the next generation. I once wrote such a letter to my godly grandmother only to discover later that my grandfather was reading it aloud to all of the visitors who came to their home!

So, consider extending your ministry by writing occasional articles or pastoral reflections for your congregation and community. If you do, write personally and candidly – these are the stories that find eager readers. Church members will ponder your ideas for a longer time if they can hold them in their hands. Imagine what our lives might be like if the Apostle Paul had never put his thoughts on paper (or papyrus). We'd be missing about half of the New Testament!

Good reading and good writing can help you expand your ministry. The ideas you take into your mind will influence your own thoughts. The ideas you write about will influence the thoughts of others. Even in an age of terrorism, the pen is indeed mightier than the sword.

Blessings,

Ervin

Scripture: 2 Timothy 4:11-13; 1 John 2:7-8.

Ervin R. Stutzman is academic dean at Eastern Mennonite Seminary, Harrisonburg, Va. He is also an associate professor of Church Ministries for EMS, moderator for the newly formed Mennonite Church USA, and a frequent author.

Stoking the embers:
Building your family

Dr. Myron S. Augsburger, *Be a presence for Christ*

Chuck Buller, *Jesus is not a killjoy*

Leonard Dow, *Personal financial accountability is crucial*

John M. Drescher, *Solid marriage, solid family*

Greg Funk, *We are made for eternity*

Doug Habegger, *Setting ministry boundaries*

Dorothea Janzen, *"...but we were content."*

Mike Weber, *Your ministry is your family, too*

Be a presence for Christ

By Dr. Myron S. Augsburger

While we receive many benefits from travel, it's important to be aware that travel is not all glamour. Wherever we are, we are servants of Christ and of others. One should not unduly push on doors to open. Rather, we need to be good stewards of our gifts and let God open doors of service. If we don't enjoy serving Christ at home where we are, we will hardly find fulfillment in serving him anywhere else. The key is to concentrate on being a presence for Christ and his kingdom wherever we are – at home or in our travels.

A large part of my ministry since 1951 has involved traveling. First in revival and evangelistic preaching missions, with invitations that took me across North America. Then in tent revivals and, later, in citywide missions. In my role as president of Eastern Mennonite College, I traveled to bring education and evangelism together. As a husband and father, I made special time for my family with mini-vacations. My wife, Esther, and I often spent several days of priority time together with our children, away from the distractions of work.

The amount of traveling we did was unusual – we visited more than 50 countries and many cultures. Through our traveling, we have learned to meet people where they are, to contextualize the Gospel, and to serve with compassion. The multi-denominational settings called for integrity in the presentation of the Gospel and in interpreting the Scriptures. I learned that one can be true to the Anabaptist faith and at the same time be understanding and considerate of others.

An important passage, which clarifies priorities for the traveler, is 2 Corinthians 5:15-21. We live for Christ and for others, not for ourselves. As persons reconciled with God, we can become agents of reconciliation. Our highest calling is to be ambassadors for Christ. A related passage and special favorite is Ephesians 2:14-22. This passage interfaces the evangel and the social as aspects of the Gospel. In sharing the peace of Christ's cross we can share his word of reconciliation, of justice and of peace. Whether we travel or stay at home, personal integrity in our lives is important as disciples of Christ.

Blessings,

Myron

Scripture: 2 Corinthians 5:15-2; Ephesians 2:14-22.

Myron S. Augsburger has served in many contexts, from the local church to international evangelistic preaching missions, including many ecumenical efforts across the United States and Canada. He has served as an evangelist, church planter, and pastor, as well as the moderator of his denomination – the Mennonite Church USA. He is the author of 20 books and many articles.

Jesus is not a killjoy

By Chuck Buller

The need for friends is obvious. God made us in his image (Genesis 1:27), and his image is one of relationship. Father, Son, and Spirit are the three parts of one whole. While separate in function, they are necessary for the Godhead to be completely functional in the universe.

People are like that, too. While separate as created beings, we require others to complete us and make us whole. Of course, there are always a few "lone rangers" who prefer to be by themselves most of the time, but the vast majority of us desire to live in social environments that include good relationships, interaction, and downright fun! We were created as social beings.

Now, the preferences we each have for how we socialize are as many as there are people. There are often common denominators such as food, conversation, recreation, or travel; but the most basic element is as Jesus said, "two or three gather in my name (Matthew 18:20)." For Christians, there is the unique reality that our social life is lived under the Lordship of Jesus. As such, the sky is the limit for how we have fun, who we have fun with, and even what it might cost — as long as we consider that everything we do, we do in his name.

When I was a teenager my mother used to say to me, whenever I left the house for a night out with my friends, that I should remember, "Jesus will be going along." At the time, I remember thinking that might be a real deal-breaker for fun. Yet, Jesus was not a killjoy in his time on earth, and he was a social being. He associated with all types of people, attended all types of parties, even risked a reputation that was not really becoming of his true self. Why? He did so because he loved all people and, more importantly, had a "first love" with his Father that ordered everything else in his life. As a

Christian, remember that if you seek God first, then you can live with a wide parameter of friends, social settings, and civic engagements. If you truly love God, then you can and should love your neighbors as yourself (Galatians 5:14). We should have more fun!

Blessings,

Chuck

Scripture: Genesis 1:27; Matthew 18:20; Galatians 5:14.

Chuck Buller is executive director of the Mennonite Brethren Church. He has served as a pastor and church planter in congregations in both the United States and Canada.

Personal financial accountability is crucial

By Leonard Dow

I believe as leaders in our ministries, financial accountability from a biblical standpoint must begin at home. I have rarely seen an individual whose personal finances were in disarray, whose ministry wasn't adversely affected. We who are pastors, bishops, conference ministers, and other leaders, must take the lead in managing our financial resources before we begin providing leadership to our church congregations and/or ministry programs.

I don't mean to imply those in leadership must be perfectly balanced in all financial matters. However, we must model in our finances what we desire to have in our ministries and our parishioners. It is important to be able to recognize financial bondage – but it is equally important to know how to achieve financial freedom. Financial freedom manifests itself in every aspect of a Christian's life – freedom from worry and stress about overdue bills, a clear conscience ready to focus on God and others, as well as the absolute assurance that God is in control. Because many leaders and laypeople are tormented by personal financial crises, I firmly believe the church is unable to be as effective as it could be.

Our solution is to let God manage our finances according to his holy word. As we grow in being accountable to God and his financial plans and purposes, we will become free from financial bondage. The church in Acts is a biblical model of financial freedom. In it we see the outpouring of the Holy Spirit at Pentecost. The power that accompanied this anointing brought, among other things, a high level of financial accountability in the community of believers. This community shared everything they had with one another. The text tells us that those who had land or houses willingly shared the profits from the sale of their land and would bring it to the apostles to distribute. The early church understood that all they had belonged to God. They were, in a real sense, called to simply manage their earthly resources.

Acts: 4:34 says, "There were no needy … among them. From time to time those who owned lands or houses sold them, brought the money from the sales, and put it at the apostles' feet, and it was distributed to anyone as he had need."

In my life, much of my financial difficulties were self-inflicted. Circumstances where I mistook a "want" or "desire" as an immediate "need." I have come to realize that biblical self-control and obedience are necessary parts of God's economy. Lack of self-control affects the spiritual life and manifests itself in other aspects of our lives: an inconsistent or nonexistent prayer life, reluctant study of the Bible, and minimal small group or church attendance, for example. Likewise, a lack of self-control will also have a drastic impact on our personal, as well as ministry, finances.

Biblical model for financial accountability

In Acts 5:1-11, we see that our personal finances (what we do with what we are entrusted with) is serious business (in fact, financial irresponsibility is the first recorded sin of the new church):

"Then Peter said, 'Ananias, how is it that Satan has so filled your heart that you have lied to the Holy Spirit and have kept for yourself some of the money you received for the land? Didn't it belong to you before it was sold? And after it was sold, wasn't the money at your disposal? What made you think of doing such a thing? You have not lied to men but to God.' " (Acts 5:3-4)

Ananias and Sapphira made the mistake many of us make in the area of personal finances. We fail to recognize that all things belong to God. Thus, similar to Ananias and Sapphira, we live a lie. "The earth is the Lord's, and everything in it, the world, and all who live in it." (Psalm 24:1) Each of us must choose what firstfruits we are going to set aside for God, but to make it appear we have given all when we have not (as Ananias and Sapphira did) is sinful.

If the intent of Ananias and Sapphira was to give only part of their earnings, they should've been honest and not allowed Satan to lead them to lie. As a result, both Ananias and Sapphira were held accountable and died.

Who are you accountable to in the area of your personal finances? We as parents, pastors, and church leaders, must first become knowledgeable of our finances (at home). Then, like those in the early church, we must create ways that we can be accountable (and extend grace) first to one another in our church communities, and then, foremost, to God.

Blessings,

Leonard

Scriptures: Acts 4:34; Acts 5:1-11; Psalm 24:1.

Leonard Dow is senior pastor of Oxford Circle Mennonite Church in Philadelphia, Pa., where he has served for the last five years. He is a graduate of Eastern Mennonite University and is currently working on his M.Div. at Eastern Baptist Theological Seminary. Prior to pastoring, he worked in retail banking 12 years.

Solid marriage, solid family

By John M. Drescher

In my early years of ministry, God led me to plan what became known as "Family Month." In one month, I covered, as a pastor, 30 subjects that related to the family, from birth to death. When people came to me saying things like, "Oh, I wish we had something like this when our family was young," I knew I had hit on a real need.

Since no church is stronger than its families – and if the families are not making it, the church is not making it – I'm happy I was led early to give special attention to the family. In fact, I would place even more emphasis on preventative care if I had it to do over. The early and middle childhood years are especially crucial for marriage and for parenting.

In speaking about parent-child relationships, I have come to see that the primary relationship is the one between husband and wife. That partnership is permanent; parenting is passing. So keep the partnership in good repair, and the parenting will take pretty good care of itself. The child is enriched when his or her parents live in love and demonstrate that love before their children. Plus, with that undergirding, the step to know God's love and the true meaning of human love will be sure and easy for the child. If, however, this love is not felt and seen, one can do little, many times, to teach the meaning of God's love and the true meaning of human love.

That is why I believe Scripture says so little about parent-child relationships and places the emphasis on the parents' relationship to God and to each other. For example, in Deuteronomy 6:4-9, the emphasis is upon parents being right with God themselves and then passing on the torch of faith to their children. This is also emphasized in the Proverbs and in Psalm 78:1-8, Psalms 127 and 128, Ephesians 5:21- 6:4, and Colossians 3:18-21.

All this has primary implications for spiritual leaders. It is essential that those who lead God's people keep their own relationship with their spouse vital, satisfying, and growing. I've known too many wonderful pastors whose ministry fell apart or became ineffective because they failed to keep their relationship with their spouse strong, loving, and primary. The priorities of God, family, and work are primary – particularly for us as pastors – in the building of our own family relationships. If any one of these gets out of order, all three will be in trouble and will make us ineffective in our families as well as in our service to God's family.

Blessings,

John

Scripture: Deuteronomy 6:4-9; Proverbs; Psalm 78:1-8; Psalms 127 and 128; Ephesians 5:21- 6:4; and Colossians 3:18-21.

John M. Drescher is a retired Mennonite pastor from Quakertown, Pa.

We are made for eternity

By Greg Funk

I was raised on a farm. This reality influenced my time management not only in terms of hours spent, but what I did with those hours. Early in my ministry, I worked far too much and measured productivity in terms of what I accomplished. Through the years this obsession about "doing" yielded to a more balanced perspective which included "being."

We are made for eternity. But our current view of time cannot comprehend that. Time is without bias or prejudice. It treats everyone equally. We do not manage time, but rather attempt to fill it with meaningful things. I have found encouragement in Paul's words, "You see, just at the right time . . ." (Romans 5:6) God's timing is perfect. Adopting this philosophical approach helps me relax and be patient when things do not go according to my timetable. When I realize that my time is in God's hands, not mine, it helps me to take time to listen and observe what is around me. It is in this unhurried listening that I can sort out priorities and act accordingly.

Wow, it almost sounds like I have this time thing all worked out! Believe me, I do not. I'm learning I still need to make time for other people and for myself. I'm learning I need time for silence – as well as time for the noise of our culture. I'm learning that time is more about being than it is doing.

Blessings,

Greg

Scripture: Romans 5:6.

Greg Funk is the senior pastor of Manheim (Pa.) Brethren in Christ Church.

Setting ministry boundaries

By Doug Habegger

Early on, I found I had to learn to balance ministry responsibilities with my responsibilities to my wife, Joy, and our children. Feeling the tug of ministry duties and sensing the need to spend time with my two young children often resulted in Joy getting the crumbs of my time and attention – and in spite of that, she was gracious and understanding. I should have been more aware of her needs, but I was occupied (and often preoccupied) with the demands of ministry to the extent I wasn't as available as I should have been.

There are times when I have to say "no" or "not now" to ministry demands and recognize that I need to give time and energy to our marriage. There are times when you will need to be able to do this, also. I am getting better, I think, at listening to Joy when she tells me someone else can take my place or that an "urgent" request for my time can wait. People in our congregation are very understanding when it comes to time for family and marriage. The pressure I felt early on was mostly self-imposed. It didn't come from them. I now know that they have been understanding all along. I just didn't give them enough credit for knowing that I needed time to nurture the health of our marriage.

Now that our children are grown and married, Joy and I are able to serve together in ways that were not possible when the kids were much younger. Sharing in ministry experiences with my wife has been a satisfying chapter in our role as husband and wife.

I particularly like Ephesians 5:21-33, which reminds me that I need to love my wife as Christ loves the church.

One piece of advice: Listen to your spouse! Give your spouse the right to give you input into realistic ministry boundaries. Your spouse understands that there are times and circumstances when you have no choice but to give priority to ministry demands. However, that will be understood even better if your spouse sees you making an effort to balance ministry with marriage. Finally, work hard at ministry, and work hard at marriage (Colossians 3:23). Those to whom you minister won't begrudge you time with your mate if they know you are devoted to serving them wholeheartedly.

Blessings,

Doug

Scripture: Ephesians 5:21-33; Colossians 3:23.

Doug Habegger is senior pastor of Grace Evangelical Church, Morton, Ill., which is a member of the Fellowship of Evangelical Churches. He and Joy have been married 33 years.

"...but we were content."

By Dorothea Janzen

We live in an age of greed and accumulation. Contentment is rarely mentioned as a positive virtue, yet it has been an important part of our spiritual journey through the years.

As a newly married couple, my husband and I lived in one small room at seminary with just enough space for a bed, a dresser, and a desk. We shared a bathroom with other couples who lived on our hall. We owned no car and barely had enough money to keep my husband, Heinz, in school. I worked for New York City Mission Society in a church in one of the most depressed areas of New York City and earned a small salary. Our first Christmas tree was the top cut off the tree bought for the church. I dragged it home on the subway and we set it up in our little room. My, how we enjoyed our first Christmas together with this scraggly Christmas tree. We were content!

Our first congregation owned a beautiful parsonage. After the one room at seminary it seemed as if we were living in a castle! We were so pleased to have our first real home, and we began our family of three children. But we had a salary which, even in those days, was inadequate. However, with careful planning and shopping, we always had good, if simple, food on the table. There were many things we did without, but we were content.

Through the years as we served other churches and church institutions, we were able to eventually buy a small home and provide for our children's education. There were times of struggle to meet the needs of our growing family, but somehow our needs were met. With our children all launched, we were able to save for the first time in our lives.

Now in retirement, we are quite comfortable and are able to give generously to the work of God's kingdom. "The lines have fallen for us in pleasant places." (Psalm 16:6) We are content with moving to this next step on life's journey and to see our retirement as "Sabbath time." We sometimes wonder how we ended up with so much comfort when we had so many years of eking out an existence. But as we look back, we realize that at each stage of our lives we were content with what we had. We experienced a deep sense of God's care in times when we had little and times when we had plenty.

There are several Scriptures that have helped us as we are encouraged to be content with what we have. In Philippians 4:11, we read "for I have learned to be content with whatever I have. I know what it is to have little, and I know what it is to have plenty. In any and all circumstances I have learned the secret of being well-fed and of going hungry, of having plenty and being in need. I can do all things through him who strengthens me." The writer of Hebrews says much the same thing. "Keep your lives free from the love of money and be content with what you have; for he has said, 'I will never leave you or forsake you'. So we can say with confidence, 'The Lord is my helper; I will not be afraid.'"

It takes courage to live against the grain of our culture and to eschew greed and the constant desire for more. But true peace and serenity come to those who are content with their circumstances and remember God's great faithfulness, for "all we have needed God's hand has provided."

Blessings,
Dorothea

Scripture: Philippians 4:11; Hebrews 13:15.

Dorothea Janzen is retired. She served most recently as interim pastor at Alexanderwohl Church in Goessel, Kan., and has also been an associate pastor at Bethel College Mennonite Church and co-pastor at Trinity Mennonite Church, Hillsboro, Kan.

Your ministry is your family, too

By Mike Weber

As I approach 24 years of fulfilling marriage, 23 years of active ministry, and 21 years of rewarding parenting, I can testify that it is possible to manage all three arenas and still remain (reasonably) sane. In no particular order, here is an abbreviated list of some values my wife, Nancy, and I established from the start – as well as some lessons we've learned along the way.

Keep your home *marriage*-centered, not just child-centered. Once the nest is empty, the roost returns to the way it began – just you two birds. In the interim, set aside adequate time to talk and touch – just the two of you.

"PK" does not mean "Perfect Kids." Be realistic about expectations in your family and in the church. Remember, your children have *you* for a parent. This should prompt much compassion and prayer on your part. (Ephesians 6:1-4)

Crisis time ministry. At times, a crisis in the church will call you away from a scheduled activity in your home. If so, serve willingly without whining. God can use such events to teach your children that no family exists just for itself.

Model marriage. One of the best gifts you can give your congregation, and your family, is to model a strong marriage. (Ephesians 5:25) However, if you should miss that mark, you can then model a recovering marriage – a redeemed one.

Be tactful in sharing sensitive family incidents in messages. A chuckle in the pews can lead to an icy silence around the dinner table. Depending on the age of your children, get their permission first – they were not born to be walking sermon illustrations. Always get your spouse's permission – or that icy silence around the table could spread.

Ministry is like few other occupations in that your day is never "done." It can become your life. Yet Colossians 3:4 says that *Christ* is our life. In addition to being a spouse, a parent, and a pastor, be sure to protect time for being an adopted child of *the* Father.

Blessings,

Mike

Scripture: Ephesians 6:1-4, 5:25; Colossians 3:4.

Mike Weber is the senior pastor of New Song Community Church in Elkhart, Ind., a Brethren Church. He has been a pastor for 25 years in Michigan, Illinois, and Indiana.

Sharing the warmth:

Empowering
your congregation

Dr. Curtis E. Alexander, *Encourage others to excel*

David Boshart, *Creating a place of safety*

John H. Denlinger, *To know Christ*

Dave Engbrecht, *What it doesn't have to be!*

Natalie A. Francisco, *Worship in spirit and in truth*

Ken Hunn, *Develop a heart for missions*

Elmer Lehman, *Building community*

James F. Myer, *A little 'perspiration' begets inspiration*

Phil Whetstone, *Learning to let God lead*

Larry J. Wilson, *Church finances: Keep the integrity*

Levi Ziegler, *A natural extension of life*

Encourage others to excel

By Dr. Curtis E. Alexander

Early on in my ministry, I relied too much on myself. I knew intellectually that I had some spiritual gifts and not others, but I often felt I could do most ministries better than others. Because of this, I often failed to include others in their areas of giftedness to the extent I should have. Not surprisingly, this eventually led to my own burnout, and I failed at the important task of helping others take ownership for the ministries of the church. This sometimes led to a lack of success for important ministries within the Body of Christ.

One of the things I learned is that pastors, too, are susceptible to failure in ministries when they are working outside their areas of giftedness. It's important to learn that it is okay for other people to do things better than you. In fact, it is vital for the success of ministry and for the long-term spiritual health of the individuals who are discovering, developing, and deploying their own gifts.

The fear you may need to overcome is the insecurity of realizing (and allowing others to realize) that you are not the best person to do everything. The most successful pastors find people who are gifted at a particular ministry and help them hone their ministry skills. Then the pastor will find ways to plug them into their perfect place of service. There is simply no downside to that – it's a win-win situation.

1 Corinthians 12 is a great place to understand and line up with spiritual giftedness. Also 1 Peter 4:10, which tells us to be administrators of God's grace. *Grace*, not incidentally, has the same linguistic root as the word for *spiritual gifts*. If we are intent on being grace dispensers, we will please God and succeed in ministry beyond our own expectations.

Ask God for the personal security to let others excel in their areas of giftedness while you excel in yours. Find out what you do best, then do it.

If it means that people criticize, you can explain your ministry in light of 1 Corinthians 12 and 1 Peter 4:10. If people do not understand a biblical view of spiritual gifts and ministry, then they will benefit from in-depth Bible teaching on spiritual gifts.

Blessings,

Curtis

Scripture: 1 Corinthians 12; 1 Peter 4:10.

Dr. Curtis E. Alexander is the senior pastor of Groveland (Ill.) Missionary Church and teaches world religions at Heartland Community College, Bloomington, Ill. He also teaches leadership development online for Taylor University and is the associate editor of the Missionary Church magazine, "Missionary Church Today."

Creating a place of safety

By David Boshart

"Speaking the truth in love, we must grow up in every way into him who is the head, into Christ, from whom the whole body is joined and knit together by every ligament with which it is equipped, as each part is working properly, promotes the body's growth in building itself up in love."
Ephesians 4:15-16 (NRSV)

In my first pastorate, I served a church that dealt with conflict in healthy and open ways. There was little sense that a conflict would result in broken relationships. Some time later I moved to a congregation that had experienced a lengthy and very hurtful period of conflict. This was the time in the church when the idea of pastor being a "non-anxious presence" was coming into vogue. The congregation had a lot of anxiety about conflict and a strong impulse to always smooth things over. Being a rather inexperienced pastor, I allowed my own anxiety about conflict to interpret being a non-anxious presence as taking a step back from situations of potential conflict. I thought that by taking a step back, I could be calm while others worked out their tension.

Conflict is a given. But it is also amoral. It is not something to be avoided, nor can it be. What we do with conflict becomes the moral act. I now know that to be a helpful non-anxious presence means taking a step toward the tension, naming the tension, and creating a safe place where the tension can be worked out in open and healthy ways, rather than in hidden and destructive ways.

Healthy conflict resolution can only happen when we speak the truth in love. Paul says in Ephesians 4:15 that speaking the truth in love is how we grow up to be like Jesus. Speaking the truth in love is also the way we cultivate unity in the body. I think it is quite possible to speak the truth and break relationships. It is also possible to speak in love and be less than honest. Church leaders who call people to speak the truth in love create a safe place when conflict feels threatening. Speaking the truth in love is the way we become our creative best in times of conflict. It is the way we become the body of reconciliation that mirrors the work of Jesus on the cross.

Blessings,

David

Scripture: Ephesians 4:15.

David Boshart is pastor of West Union Mennonite Church, Parnell, Iowa. He was trained as a mediator by the Iowa Mediation Service and has worked as a mediator in numerous congregational settings. He has presented workshops on power and authority and on conflict resolution.

To know Christ

By John H. Denlinger

Do you not know? Have you not heard?
Has it not been told to you from the very beginning?
Have you not understood since the earth was created?
The Lord is the everlasting God…
The fear of the Lord is the beginning of wisdom…
Be still and know that I am the Lord your God…
Knowledge puffs up but love builds up…

— Selected Scriptures

Christian education has been happening since the beginning of time. To know Christ has always been a primary focus of the church of Jesus Christ. God informed and instructed his people to teach their children well.

> *"You must commit yourselves wholeheartedly to these commands I am giving you today. Repeat them again and again to your children. Talk about them when you are at home and when you are away on a journey, when you are lying down and when you are getting up again. Tie them to your hands as a reminder, and wear them on your forehead. Write them on the doorposts of your house and on your gates." (Deuteronomy 6:6-9)*

In other words, pass on the faith – pass on the knowledge of God and of God's journey with his people.

As an educator for nearly 20 years in school and in university, I often viewed formal education in the classroom as the way to form, transform, conform, and reform ourselves into the image of God as we were created to be.

As a pastor, I have grown to see and understand more clearly that the formal classroom must partner with and reflect the classroom of our homes and churches. The writer of Ecclesiastes tells us a three-fold cord is not easily broken. As the home, church, and school cooperate, education is at its best. Information becomes instructive.

I believe education is more "caught" than taught, and one should not let a formal classroom setting interfere too much with the total educational experience that occurs outside the classroom. There's an old aphorism it would be good, as pastors, to remember: "Most people don't care how much you know unless they first know how much you care." This is an important reminder as we educate and is especially true in this age of information.

Education, in the church and in life, is a continuing process where God, as the potter, shapes and molds us, his clay (Isaiah 64:8). God fills us as jars of clay to reveal the treasure of Jesus Christ who is in us, so that others may come to know Jesus and the love of God.

As we come into the presence of God daily to listen, to learn, to know God, and to be a living sacrifice, we are changed by the renewing of our minds in Christ Jesus. We are transformed, not conformed, into the person God wants us to be – into a new creature.

Now we see dimly: some day we will see clearly. Until then, it is our prayer to know God more clearly, to follow God more nearly, and to love God (and others as myself) more dearly, day by day.

Blessings,

John

Scriptures: Deuteronomy 6:6-9; Romans 12:1-2; Isaiah 64:8.

John H. Denlinger is pastor of Ridgeview Mennonite Church, Gordonville, Pa., which is part of the Atlantic Coast Conference of Mennonite Church USA. John has taught and coached at public and private high schools and at Eastern Mennonite University. He has served on the executive board of Lancaster Mennonite School.

What it doesn't have to be!

By Dave Engbrecht

Early in ministry, I was enslaved to the urgent at the expense of the important. The demands of pastoring and all of its accompanying duties consumed all my energy. It wasn't until I saw the tyranny of the urgent that I was motivated to invest in long-term planning. Strategic planning caused the creative juices to flow! Vision became the fuel for ministry, and capturing a picture of the preferred future energized the entire church body. What *was* didn't have to *be*! It is possible to navigate the streams of change through intentional long-term strategic planning with broad-based congregational ownership.

Ownership of the vision is essential for strategic planning to work. No one enjoys it when something is done *to* them – the preferred method is for it to be done *with* them. While that process is laborious and often frustrating, the momentum gained from it can be unstoppable. Key people, those who are big-picture thinkers, are best at authoring the strategic plan with periodic input from a broad-based leadership group. However, it is important that the key players not get too far ahead of the congregation or they will be mistaken for the enemy.

The best strategic plans are integrated with a timeline that becomes a guide to what needs to happen when. This timeline also provides built-in accountability and an objective standard to keep implementation of the strategy on track.

Proverbs 21:31 ought to be a guiding principle in this process. "The horse is made ready for the day of battle, but victory rests with the Lord!" We have no right to expect victory if we do not prepare adequately. Yet adequate preparation without the anointing of the Lord is pointless. Yes, those who "fail to plan, plan to fail." Long-term strategic planning creates an air of excitement and anticipation. It fosters an attitude that says, "Our greatest days are just ahead!"

Blessings,

Dave

Scripture: Proverbs 21:31.

Dave Engbrecht is senior pastor of Nappanee (Ind.) Missionary Church, which, through long-term planning, has grown from a church with an average attendance of 124 in 1979, to a body of believers currently 2,650 strong.

Worship in spirit and in truth

By Natalie A. Francisco

I knew when I was five years old that I had a passion for music. My continued persistence, insistence, with the idea of learning to play the piano, touched my mother's heart. In response, she purchased a piano seven years later. At this same time, I received Jesus Christ as Savior and became a member of Calvary Mennonite Church in Newport News, Va.

My passion for music stemmed from an even greater calling on my life, as I would later discover. At age 12, I asked the pastor of the church (the late Bishop Leslie Francisco) to anoint my hands with oil and to pray for me to receive the gift of playing the piano. At the time, there was a great need for someone to accompany the worship leader and to direct the choirs of the church. I promised God I would always use my life to glorify him, if he would trust me with this special gift.

Childlike faith was all that was needed for the purposes of God to be manifested in my life. Within six months, I found that I could play any song I heard, and I would soon accompany and direct the worship team, choirs, and soloists in the church. God's plan for me also included marrying the pastor's son, Leslie W. Francisco III, who would later become my bishop/pastor and employer.

The *ministry* of music and worship remains my passion to this day. However, I have come to understand the *meaning* of worship extends far beyond a liturgical order of service or a segment of songs performed before an audience. Worship encompasses one's lifestyle – the inward expressions of the heart and mind, as well as the outward expressions of one's conversation and conduct. Worship involves dedicating one's time, talents, and treasures to God in an effort to serve him wholeheartedly. Music, then, is just one small piece of what is to be devoted to God as an act of worship. Every minute of every day should be viewed as worship as we, God's children, seek to glorify him with our lives.

My favorite Scripture concerning worship is John 4:23-24 (NKJV). *"But the hour is coming, and now is, when the true worshipers will worship the Father in spirit and truth; for the Father is seeking such to worship Him. God is Spirit, and those who worship Him must worship in spirit and truth."* This passage reminds me that my heavenly Father desires, and is looking for, those who will worship and serve him with the essence of who they are as well as with all he has entrusted to them.

I have had the privilege of singing and teaching the gospel across the United States as well as in Jamaica, Ghana, and South Africa. I have experienced the expressions of worship in many different ethnic/cultural settings, and as a result, I have come to appreciate various styles of vocal and instrumental music. All of us can learn from each other as we attempt to amalgamate the unique harmonies of extemporaneous singing with the four-part harmony of acappella singing in our hymns and choruses. Another favorite Scripture passage is Zephaniah 3:9-12, which reminds me that God desires to receive all worship, as long as it is pure.

Worship is not one more thing to add to your daily "to do" list, as you might add Bible study, prayer, or singing. Instead, worship is all that you say and do each day. I encourage you to commit your thoughts, words, and deeds to God as your daily act of worship. Then, your reason for living becomes to honor God out of a sense of reverence rather than duty or obligation. True worship involves the total, freewill offering of yourself to God in a relationship of mutual love and commitment. (Proverbs 16:3; Romans 12:1-2) When viewed in this light, worship is not difficult. Rather, it becomes dynamic and vibrant as you become enamored with the presence of God that floods your mind and heart.

Blessings,
Natalie

Scripture: John 4:23-24; Zephaniah 3:9-12; Proverbs 16:3; Romans 12:1-2.

Natalie A. Francisco is the administrator of programs and personnel, as well as minister of music, at Calvary Mennonite Church, Newport News, Va. With her husband, she has recorded a CD, "We Worship You," which features the church's music ministry. She serves on the board of directors of MMA.

Develop a heart for missions

By Ken Hunn

Having just begun a new area of ministry since last July, these are my early years! It has been a steep learning curve. In Argentina, everyone greets with a cheek-to-cheek kiss. In India, the greeting consists of bringing your hands together in front of your chest, palm to palm, along with a bowed head. In the Philippines, when shaking hands, the young especially will take your hand and touch their forehead, both as a way of greeting and asking for your blessing. So there's been a lot of learning from culture to culture. This newness has stretched my mind and my soul as I learn to minister to a variety of people all at once.

My world has become a lot larger – and more diverse. Things I now experience are often seen through the lens of other people in other places. How would my friends from other parts of the world respond to the challenges and opportunities I face here in the United States? We have been blessed with many material things in our country. We need to be sure to use those blessings for God's kingdom, instead of allowing them to make us complacent or, worse, dependent on the excess that the rest of the world does without. Our brothers and sisters around the world serve Christ with a passion that surpasses their poverty. We must recapture our fervor and learn to live more sacrificially.

I find myself going more often to the Psalms. They offer direction along with inspiration, which I need more than ever in this season of my life. *Ascribe to the Lord, O families of nations, ascribe to the Lord glory and strength. Ascribe to the Lord the glory due his name; bring an offering and come into his courts. Worship the Lord in the splendor of his holiness; tremble before him all the earth.* (Psalm 96:7-9) (NIV)

Though we worship according to different cultures, our encounter with the Almighty and the offerings we bring to that experience are an incredible unifying factor.

I was a pastor for 23 years. For many of those years, I held missions at arm's length. A short-term trip to India by a group from my congregation transformed my thoughts about giving and receiving, other cultures, and people in general. This experience transformed the hearts of our entire congregation through the shared experience of those who participated in the trip. I learned that God richly blesses our efforts to unite with his heart's desire, which is that all should hear of his Son! It truly is more blessed to give than receive. Pastor, get more involved with taking the Gospel around the world, and see how God blesses you in your own neighborhood!

Blessings,

Ken

Scripture: Psalm 96:7-9.

Ken Hunn is the executive director of the Brethren Church, Ashland, Ohio, and has been a pastor for 23 years.

Building community

By Elmer Lehman

We were inexperienced church planters when we began a new work in Costa Rica. I had the illusion that by starting from scratch, we could avoid having problem people in the church by carefully choosing who we wanted – and did not want. I quickly discovered, however, that God places whom he will into the church with their various strengths and weaknesses, their idiosyncrasies, their abilities and giftings – and rightly so. Our role is to accept them, disciple them, help them to mature, and discover how their giftings and resources can be used to bless the body.

Early on, we tended to feel sorry for these people with their limited resources, and we tried to do too many things *for* them. We then discovered the joy of doing things *with* people as we partnered with them in the building of the church.

As evangelical Christians, we were a minority in the country and experienced close fellowship with other evangelical Christian groups already established there. It seemed each group had its distinct contribution to make to the overall movement of what God was doing. Pentecostals contributed a zeal for evangelism. Charismatics contributed excitement and enthusiasm in following Jesus. Baptists supplied a broad spectrum of nurturing materials. Mennonites were admired for our peace stance, our ethics, and our ministry of reconciliation – and so on. Together, we modeled Christian community.

Ephesians is a special letter with its emphasis on unity and what it means to live out community in different settings. Many pastors find themselves busy and on the verge of burnout by trying to *do* the work of the ministry. But Ephesians 4 teaches us that pastors are placed into the church to *equip* the saints for ministry. What a joy it is to help the saints develop their gifts and release those saints for ministry – thereby freeing up the pastor to continue his ministry of equipping the saints.

I recall the joy I experienced when, after giving leadership to organizing the Costa Rica Mennonite Conference and then presiding over that conference in its early years, I was able to sit back and watch a Costa Rican brother give capable leadership to the role I had relinquished. I knew the church was in good hands.

God places the gifts in the church, not for competition, not for prideful display, not as trophies nor as rewards for holiness, but as tools to be used in the work of building the church. It is vital that we discern what gifts are given to each member of the body – and that we thank God for them. God has given me gifts to bless others, and he has given others gifts to bless me. Thus, the entire body is blessed.

Blessings,

Elmer

Scripture: Select verses from Ephesians 4.

Elmer Lehman was a church planter for many years and is now an overseer in the Mennonite Church (Conservative Mennonite Conference).

A little 'perspiration' begets inspiration

By James F. Myer

I did not volunteer for the ministry.

When first called to the ministry at age 22 through a congregational election/discernment process, I was particularly concerned about being "clean" from all past offenses and sins. So I made it my business to go around and visit a few of my peers who had been along during my teenage years and who had, with me, engaged in some conduct that was less than honorable.

I simply asked forgiveness for any way that I had influenced them in the wrong direction. Doing this was not easy, but it removed all the skeletons from my closet that I feared would show up to haunt me sometime when I was teaching or preaching God's word. My early challenge was to be a personal example with my life about the things that I would be sharing later through public speaking.

I remember as a young pastor being struck by the fact that the next sermon or class presentation is always facing you. In spite of the sense of relief experienced after preaching a sermon or making a presentation, the next one is always close – just ahead of you. To be successful as a preacher requires disciplined study habits and preparation. It is still true that some "perspiration" in your study will result in greater "inspiration" in your pulpit.

It is important to always be working on your public speaking skills. Among all the other things a minister is called upon to do, nothing is more important than presenting an easy-to-listen-to sound and a well-researched biblical message to the congregation. Many of today's church members have been entertained all week long by professional media presentations, so Sunday "dry bones" preaching will not cut it. Sermons ought to have a real-life flavor as well as be a bit entertaining. Using a sprinkling of appropriate humor helps relax an audience and encourages them to agree with you. I maintain a growing list of humorous illustrations to help maintain audience attention. Some Scriptures relevant to the call to minister include:

- **The Call of Moses** – Exodus 3
- **The Commissioning of Isaiah** – Isaiah 6
- **The Needs of the Multitude** – Matthew 9:35-38
- **The Ordaining of the Twelve** – Mark 2:13-19
- **The Inspiration of the Bible** – 2 Timothy 3:14-16
- **The Challenge to Study and be Diligent** – 2 Timothy 2:15 and 1 Timothy 4:12-16
- **The Satisfaction of a Completed Ministry** – 2 Timothy 4:6-8

Keep yourself spiritually motivated and stimulated. Quickly clicking from the computer a few fabulous paragraphs of information that you easily paste onto your sermon will not likely give spiritual benefit to yourself – or your congregation – over the long haul. All of us need regular devotional practices that feed our souls. So don't spend so much time playing with the computer or even watching television.

Keep yourself physically energized. Have regular appointments with the doctor, and take the medicine and exercise advice he or she suggests. One doctor told a deacon brother, "If you will walk one mile a day, you will never have a nervous breakdown." I've been following this regimen recently, and the result is better blood tests. Jesus also needed some time away from the crowds. Be encouraged with some words from Paul, "The one who calls you is faithful and He will also do it." (1 Thessalonians 5:24)

Blessings,

James

Scripture: Exodus 3; Isaiah 6; Matthew 9:35-38; Mark 2:13-19; 1 Timothy 4:12-16; 2 Timothy 2:15, 3:14-16, 4:6-8; 1 Thessalonians 5:24.

James F. Myer is a minister of White Oak Church of the Brethren, Manheim, Pa., and has served as moderator of the denomination's annual conference. He is also a farmer.

Learning to let God lead

By Phil Whetstone

My early years in ministry and leadership was like most people's: I was clueless. My education didn't prepare me for the endurance level needed for weekly consistency. As a result, I had a low tolerance level for the pain of ministry. Setbacks were seen as failures, and disappointments easily became discouragements.

The lessons I've been learning since still aren't fully developed, but there are *five* thoughts that hold me steady, that the Lord has given to me through his ministry to me, and that I want to share with you.

1. **The roots grow the deepest where the wind blows the strongest.** An observation of this lesson from nature is pretty clear. Botany teaches that trees subjected to the pressure of high winds grow their roots deeper in order to stand secure. They may not be pretty, but they are strong. Scripture teaches the same principle on tough times in leadership. The battles that seem so strong right now will be the soil God uses to build you into the pastor he wants you to be. (Romans 5:1-5)

2. **God never called me to be successful; he called me to be faithful.** My job is not to determine or manufacture success. My job is to remain faithful to the call God has for my life. He determines the success of our ministry. (1 Thessalonians 5:23-24; 1 Corinthians 3:5-9; 2 Corinthians 4:7-12)

3. **That which is attempted in the flesh can only yield the flesh.** Only that which is attempted by the Spirit, can yield the eternal. My strength hasn't accomplished anything of eternal value. Only the Holy Spirit can change a heart and bring about true fruit. You mustn't forget that. (John 3:5-7)

4. **I will make it through.** If the difficulties of the past have taught me anything, it is that God will not abandon me. He will see me through to the other side. It may not come as quickly as I want, but God is always on time. He always provides the right way and in the right amount. (Joshua 1; 1 Kings 17:7-15)

5. **I'm not alone.** Others have gone through what you will be going through. The old statement "Misery loves company" is only partly true. Misery needs company."

I gain great strength knowing that the Apostle Paul, too, felt abandoned, alone, frustrated, and hurt. Paul knew what he was saying when he said, "endure," because he had to endure and abide under the load. When he said, "No temptation has seized you except what is common to man," he could very well have said, "tough time" or "trial" instead of "temptation." The fact that others have gone through these trials and are praying me through is a great source of comfort. (2 Timothy 4:6-18; 1 Corinthians 10:13; 2 Corinthians 6:11-13 and 7:2-4)

Often, going through a particular stretch of difficulty, I couldn't tell if I was under attack or under God's discipline. But, I finally got on my knees and said, "Lord, I don't know if the enemy is attacking or if you are trying to get my attention. If it's the enemy, I come against him in the strong name of Jesus Christ, and if you are trying to get my attention – I'm listening."

To this day, I don't know which it was, but I know that as soon as I quit wallowing in the problem and began celebrating God's presence, my outlook changed. Hold firm, and listen hard. The greatest victory is usually around the corner.

Blessings,

Phil

Scripture: Romans 5:1-5; 1 Thessalonians 5:23-24; 1 Corinthians 3:5-9, 10:13; 2 Corinthians 4:7-12, 16-18; 6:11-13, 7:2-4; John 3:5-7; Joshua 1; 1 Kings 17:7-15; 2 Timothy 4:6-18, 7:2-4; Isaiah 43:2-3, 4.

Phil Whetstone is the senior pastor of Colonial Woods Missionary Church, Port Huron, Mich.

Church finances: Keep the integrity

By Larry J. Wilson

I have always been blessed to work with lay leaders who have had more experience and knowledge of how finances and budgets in the church came together. Their wisdom and success in helping the congregation meet or exceed its budget goals is something I chose not to tamper with.

At my churches, we always met our giving targets. What is harder to recall is how those targets were set. Generally speaking, the church treasurer and finance committee created the budgets. Then the church council adjusted their figures. Finally, after much discussion, the members of the congregation voted.

Over my 38 years in ministry, this pattern has followed me wherever I've gone. Of course, there were times when we tried to get the congregation more involved earlier in the budgeting process, but there generally was not much interest. One thing I've never tried, but that seems like a good idea, is a narrative spending plan.

Though I personally enjoy giving, and it is definitely a part of my walk with Christ, only occasionally do I use personal examples with regard to giving or spending choices in conversation or in sermons. I like to think I'm comfortable talking about money, but really I'm not. My personal giving is more than a tithe – and I'd like to give even more – but I am concerned about saving for my retirement years (is that a lack of faith?). My wife and I give separately, out of our respective salaries, and though we give differently, we both feel good about how it's done.

At (our present congregation) we have used Sunday school classes and church retreats to talk about lifestyles, money, spending choices, and so on.

I would like to believe this translates over into all aspects of our lives – and for many, it has. However, in glancing over the past year's giving at church, I was surprised that five to seven of my families carried way too much of the budget, while some gave very little (this was not tied to income). So there is still much more education and talking that ought to be going on here. I'd like to believe many of these folks are giving outside the church budget, which is likely for some, but I don't know that to be the case.

One of our small groups did set up an accountability group, sharing with each other regarding their personal/family finances. But that has been the exception rather than the rule. We have made our congregational offering much more a part of the Sunday worship experience and that feels healthy. This includes the ushers raising the offering plates overhead – including the children's offering basket – during the prayer.

If this is an area you struggle with in your church, first be certain your own finances and priorities are in line, because this will free you in all areas of your life. Then, gather your leadership team together and collectively work on money issues – not just at budget time. Constantly connect your church finances to your congregation's mission. Monitor how much of your church budget is spent on yourselves and your own comfort – and how much is spent on the wider church and needs of others.

For integrity's sake, be certain that your church provides fair staff salaries. The denominational salary guidelines are a great gift to pastors and congregations. With your leadership team, read and discuss some of the excellent books on money that are available from Herald Press and elsewhere. Pray about all of these matters, and listen carefully to what you hear. When you think you've heard an answer, test that answer with people in your congregation who you know have the church mission near to their hearts.

Blessings,

Larry

Scriptures: Matthew 6:24-34; 1 Corinthians 16:2; 2 Corinthians 8:6-8; Philippians 4:11b-13; 1 John 3:17; Luke 18:18-30, 21:1-4.

Larry J. Wilson is the pastor of First Mennonite Church in Urbana, Ill.

A natural extension of life

By Levi Ziegler

As I began pastoral ministry in July 1956, I already had some guidance in the area of dealing with death. The man who was my pastor during my high school and college days had served as my coach in this area. The seminary also had a good professor who prepared the students to deal with death in pastoral ministry.

The first death I faced as a pastor was that of a 9-month-old baby boy who died suddenly while 18 miles from a hospital. Soon other deaths followed, including that of a prominent man in the church and community. I felt no discomfort dealing with these deaths and always knew God was with me.

The bigger challenge came when I was working with mountain families who still had their wakes, or viewings, in their homes. In many of those situations the folk were very good at providing the appropriate "weeping and wailing" during visitation and viewing, as well as at the funeral. This was new to me, and I felt the noise being made did not come from genuine grief, but rather from custom. In addition, I often worked with families where there was a feud brewing, going on, or just finishing – and the families were often divided. What a challenge!

In those early days, viewings routinely lasted for two nights and two afternoons – and this seemed, at the time, good and healthy. However, over the years I learned that giving that much time for the pre-funeral activities was very difficult on the families and really did not accomplish anything worth the suffering. So I found myself questioning the value of viewings.

In later years, I have again begun seeing the value of a viewing and the necessity of allowing families time with the deceased. There is value in friends being able to see the body and being able to mourn for a brief time with the family.

I used to see death as an enemy of people; however, I have come to realize death can be a friend to the one who is diseased, maimed for life, or totally unaware of life. Death, as I see it now, can be a friend to the one leaving this world, though, perhaps an enemy to the family left behind. The process of dying can provide valuable time for sharing between family members and the person facing death. It can provide a time of preparation for everyone and enable loved ones to give special care and love.

In my experience, Psalm 23 has been a meaningful Scripture to almost everyone involved with a death. Many find immeasurable benefit in being able to recite it from memory. In addition, 2 Corinthians 4:16-5:6 is an excellent text to share with those whose loved one's body wasted away or who lingered for a long time.

It is vital that, as a pastor, you are not afraid to be human. If a death brings tears to you personally, cry with the family – let them see your grief as you share theirs. Listen to the family carefully and closely to hear what they are really saying as they talk about their loved one and as they talk about their own needs.

Death is only the vehicle that sets the soul free from this life to enter the eternal life, and therefore, can be a friend. Death releases many from a prison in which they have lived for many years, while giving relief to those whose age is dictating to them, "time to go home."

Recognize that death is a natural extension of life and is only an enemy when the soul is not in Christ's loving care.

Blessings,

Levi

Scripture: Psalm 23, 103:8-18; Isaiah 26:3-4, 40:28-31; Matthew 11:28-30; John 14:1-6, 27; John 11:17-27; John 17:20-26; Romans 8:31-39; 1 Corinthians 15:51-58; 2 Corinthians 4:16-5:6; Job 19:23-27; Psalm 90:1, 2; 91:1, 2; 46:1, 10; 1 Thessalonians 4:13-17; Revelation 21:1-7.

Levi Ziegler is associate chaplain at Brethren Village in Manheim, Pa.